grep
Pocket Reference

grep
Pocket Reference

John Bambenek and Agnieszka Klus

Beijing · Cambridge · Farnham · Köln · Sebastopol · Tokyo

grep Pocket Reference
by John Bambenek and Agnieszka Klus

Copyright © 2009 John Bambenek and Agnieszka Klus. All rights reserved.
Printed in the United States of America.

Published by O'Reilly Media, Inc., 1005 Gravenstein Highway North, Sebastopol, CA 95472.

O'Reilly books may be purchased for educational, business, or sales promotional use. Online editions are also available for most titles (*http://safari .oreilly.com*). For more information, contact our corporate/institutional sales department: (800) 998-9938 or *corporate@oreilly.com*.

Editor: Isabel Kunkle
Copy Editor: Genevieve d'Entremont
Production Editor: Loranah Dimant
Proofreader: Loranah Dimant
Indexer: Joe Wizda
Cover Designer: Karen Montgomery
Interior Designer: David Futato

Printing History:
    January 2009:   First Edition.

ISBN: 978-0-596-15360-1

[LSI]   [2011-12-02]

1322596400

Contents

grep Pocket Reference

Introduction

Chances are that if you've worked for any length of time on a Linux system, either as a system administrator or as a developer, you've used the *grep* command. The tool is installed by default on almost every installation of Linux, BSD, and Unix, regardless of distribution, and is even available for Windows (with wingrep or via Cygwin).

GNU and the Free Software Foundation distribute *grep* as part of their suite of open source tools. Other versions of *grep* are distributed for other operating systems, but this book focuses primarily on the GNU version, as it is the most prevalent at this point.

The *grep* command lets the user find text in a given file or output quickly and easily. By giving *grep* a string to search for, it will print out only lines that contain that string and can print the corresponding line numbers for that text. The "simple" use of the command is well-known, but there are a variety of more advanced uses that make *grep* a powerful search tool.

The purpose of this book is to pack all the information an administrator or developer could ever want into a small guide that can be carried around. Although the "simple" uses of *grep* do not require much education, the advanced applications and the use of regular expressions can become quite complicated. The name of the tool is actually an acronym for "Global Regular-Expression Print," which gives an indication of its purpose.

GNU *grep* is actually a combination of four different tools, each with its unique style of finding text: basic regular expressions, extended regular expressions, fixed strings, and Perl-style regular expression. There are other implementations of *grep*-like programs such as agrep, zipgrep, and "grep-like" functions in .NET, PHP, and SQL. This guide will describe the particular options and strengths of each style.

The official website for *grep* is *http://www.gnu.org/software/grep/*. It contains information about the project and some brief documentation. The source code for *grep* is only 712 KB, and the current version at the time of this writing is 2.5.3. This pocket reference is current to that version, but the information will be generally valid for earlier and later versions.

As an important note, the current version of *grep* that ships with Mac OS X 10.5.5 is 2.5.1; however, most of the options in this book will still work for that version. There are other "grep" programs as well, in addition to the one from GNU, and these are typically the ones installed by default under HP-UX, AIX, and older versions of Solaris. For the most part, the regular expression syntax is very similar between these versions, but the options differ. This book deals exclusively with the GNU version because it is more robust and powerful than other versions.

Conventions Used in This Book

The following typographical conventions are used in this book:

Italic

> Indicates commands, new terms, URLs, email addresses, filenames, file extensions, pathnames, directories, and Unix utilities.

`Constant width`

> Indicates options, switches, variables, attributes, keys, functions, types, classes, namespaces, methods, modules, properties, parameters, values, objects, events, event handlers, XML tags, HTML tags, macros, the contents of files, or the output from commands.

`Constant width italic`

> Shows text that should be replaced with user-supplied values.

Using Code Examples

This book is here to help you get your job done. In general, you may use the code in this book in your programs and documentation. You do not need to contact us for permission unless you're reproducing a significant portion of the code. For example, writing a program that uses several chunks of code from this book does not require permission. Selling or distributing a CD-ROM of examples from O'Reilly books does require permission. Answering a question by citing this book and quoting example code does not require permission. Incorporating a significant amount of example code from this book into your product's documentation does require permission.

We appreciate, but do not require, attribution. An attribution usually includes the title, author, publisher, and ISBN. For example: "*grep Pocket Reference* by John Bambenek and Agnieszka Klus. Copyright 2009 John Bambenek and Agnieszka Klus, 978-0-596-15360-1."

If you feel your use of code examples falls outside fair use or the permission given here, feel free to contact us at *permissions@oreilly.com*.

Safari® Books Online

Safari
Books Online

When you see a Safari® Books Online icon on the cover of your favorite technology book, that means the book is available online through the O'Reilly Network Safari Bookshelf.

Safari offers a solution that's better than e-books. It's a virtual library that lets you easily search thousands of top tech books, cut and paste code samples, download chapters, and find quick answers when you need the most accurate, current information. Try it for free at *http://safari.oreilly.com*.

Comments and Questions

Please address comments and questions concerning this book to the publisher:

O'Reilly Media, Inc.
1005 Gravenstein Highway North
Sebastopol, CA 95472
800-998-9938 (in the United States or Canada)
707-829-0515 (international or local)
707-829-0104 (fax)

We have a web page for this book, where we list errata, examples, and any additional information. You can access this page at:

http://www.oreilly.com/catalog/9780596153601

To comment or ask technical questions about this book, send email to:

bookquestions@oreilly.com

For more information about our books, conferences, Resource Centers, and the O'Reilly Network, see our website at:

http://www.oreilly.com

Acknowledgments

From John Bambenek

I would like to thank Isabel Kunkle and the rest of the O'Reilly team behind the editing and production of this book. My wife and son deserve thanks for their support and love as I completed this project. My coauthor, Agnieszka, has been invaluable in making an onerous task of writing a book more manageable; she contributed greatly to this project. Brian Krebs of *The Washington Post* deserves credit for the idea of writing this book. My time at the Internet Storm Center has let me work with some of the best in the information security industry, and their feedback has been extremely helpful during the technical review process. A particular note of thanks goes out to Charles Hamby, Mark Hofman, and Donald Smith. And last, Merry Anne's Diner in downtown Champaign, Illinois deserves thanks for letting me show up for hours in the middle of the night to take up one of their tables as I wrote this.

From Agnieszka Klus

First, I want to thank my coauthor, John Bambenek, for the opportunity to work on this book. It certainly has been a literary adventure for me. It has opened windows of opportunity and given me a chance to peek into a world I would otherwise have not been able to. I also would like to thank my family and friends for their support and patience.

Conceptual Overview

The *grep* command provides a variety of ways to find strings of text in a file or stream of output. For example, it is possible to find every instance of a specified word or string in a file. This could be useful for grabbing particular log entries out of voluminous system logs, as one example. It is possible to search for certain patterns in files, such as the typical pattern of a credit card number. This flexibility makes *grep* a powerful tool for finding the presence (or absence) of information in files. There are two ways to provide input to *grep*, each with its own particular uses.

First, *grep* can be used to search a given file or files on a system. For instance, files on a disk can be searched for the presence (or absence) of specific content. *grep* also can be used to send output from another command that *grep* will then search for the desired content. For instance, *grep* could be used to pick out important information from a command that otherwise produces an excessive amount of output.

While searching text files, *grep* could be employed to search for a particular string throughout all files in an entire filesystem. For instance, Social Security numbers follow a known pattern, so it is possible to search every text file on a system to find occurrences of these numbers in its files (e.g., for academic environments in order to comply with federal privacy laws). The default behavior is to return the filename and the line of text that contains the string, but it is possible to include line numbers as well.

Additionally, *grep* can examine command output to look for occurrences of a string. For instance, a system administrator may run a script to update software on a system that has a large amount of "debugging" information and may only care to see error messages. In this case, the *grep* command could search for a string (i.e., "ERROR") that indicates errors, filtering out information that the administrator does not want to see.

Generally, the *grep* command is designed to search only text output or text files. The command will let you search binary (or other nontext) files, but the utility is limited in that regard. Tricks for searching binary files for information with *grep* (i.e., using the *strings* command) are covered in the last section ("Advanced Tips and Tricks with grep" on page 57).

Although it is usually possible to integrate *grep* into manipulating text or doing "search and replace" operations, it is not the most efficient way to get the job done. Instead, the *sed* and *awk* programs are more useful for these kinds of functions.

There are two basic ways to search with *grep*: searching for fixed strings and searching for patterns of text. Searching for fixed strings is pretty straightforward. Pattern searching, however, can get complicated very quickly, depending on how variable that desired pattern is. To search for text with variable content, use regular expressions.

Introduction to Regular Expressions

Regular expressions, the source of the letters "re" in "grep," are the foundation for creating a powerful and flexible text-processing tool. Expressions can add, delete, segregate, and generally manipulate all kinds of text and data. They are simple statements that enhance a user's ability to process files, especially when combined with other commands. If applied properly, regular expressions can significantly simplify a tall task.

Many different commands in the Unix/Linux world use some form of regular expressions in addition to some programming languages. For instance, the *sed* and *awk* commands use regular expressions not only to find information, but also to manipulate it.

There are actually many different varieties of regular expressions. For instance, Java and Perl both have their own syntax for regular expressions. Some applications have their own versions of regular expressions, such as Sendmail and Oracle. GNU *grep* uses the GNU version of regular expressions, which is very similar (but not identical) to POSIX regular expressions.

In fact, most of the varieties of regular expressions are very similar, but they do have key differences. For instance, some of the escapes, metacharacters, or special operators will behave differently depending on which type of regular expressions you are using. The subtle differences between the varieties can lead to drastically different results when using the same expression under different regular expression types. This book will only touch on the regular expressions that are used by *grep* and Perl-style *grep* (*grep* -P).

Usually, regular expressions are included in the *grep* command in the following format:

```
grep [options] [regexp] [filename]
```

Regular expressions are comprised of two types of characters: normal text characters, called *literals*, and special characters, such as the asterisk (*), called *metacharacters*. An *escape sequence* allows you to use metacharacters as literals or to identify special characters or conditions (such as word boundaries or "tab characters"). The desired string that someone hopes to find is a *target string*. A *regular expression* is the particular search pattern that is entered to find a particular target string. It may be the same as the target string, or it may include some of the regular expression functionality discussed next.

Quotation Marks and Regular Expressions

It is customary to place the regular expression (or *regxp*) inside single quotation marks (the symbol on the keyboard underneath the double quote, not underneath the tilde [~] key). There are a few reasons for this. The first is that normally Unix shells interpret the space as an end of argument and the start of a new one. In the format just shown, you see the syntax of the *grep* command where a space separates the regexp from the filename. What if the string you wish to search for has a "space" character? The quotes tell *grep* (or another Unix command) where the argument starts and stops when spaces or other special characters are involved.

The other reason is that various types of quotes can signify different things with shell commands such as *grep*. For instance, using the single quote underneath the tilde key (also called the backtick) tells the shell to execute everything inside those quotes as a command and then use that as the string. For instance:

```
grep `whoami` filename
```

would run the *whoami* command (which returns the username that is running the shell on Unix systems) and then use that string to search. For instance, if I were logged in with username "bambenek", *grep* would search *filename* for the use of "bambenek".

Double quotes, however, work the same as the single quotes, but with one important difference. With double quotes, it becomes possible to use environment variables as part of a search pattern:

```
grep "$HOME" filename
```

The environment variable HOME is normally the absolute path of the logged-in user's home directory. The *grep* command just shown would determine the meaning of the variable HOME and then search on that string. If you place $HOME in single quotes, it would not recognize it as an environment variable.

It is important to craft the regular expression with the right type of quotation marks because different types can yield wildly different results. Beginning and ending quotes must be the same or an error will be generated, letting you know that your syntax is incorrect. Note that it is possible to combine the use of different quotation marks to combine functionality. This will be discussed later in the section "Advanced Tips and Tricks with grep" on page 57.

Metacharacters

In addition to quotation marks, the position and combination of other special characters produce different effects on the regular expression. For example, the following command searches the file *name.list* for the letter 'e' followed by 'a':

```
grep -e 'e[a]' name.list
```

But by simply adding the caret symbol, ^, you change the entire meaning of the expression. Now you are searching for the 'e' followed by anything that is *not* the letter 'a':

```
grep -e 'e[^a]' name.list
```

Since metacharacters help define the manipulation, it is important to be familiar with them. Table 1 has a list of regularly used special characters and their meanings.

Table 1. Regular expression metacharacters[a]

Metacharacter	Name	Matches
Items to match a single character		
.	Dot	Any one character
[...]	Character class	Any character listed in brackets
[^...]	Negated character class	Any character not listed in brackets
\char	Escape character	The character after the slash literally; used when you want to search for a "special" character, such as "$" (i.e., use "\$")
Items that match a position		
^	Caret	Start of a line
$	Dollar sign	End of a line
\<	Backslash less-than	Start of a word
\>	Backslash greater-than	End of a word
The quantifiers		
?	Question mark	Optional; considered a quantifier
*	Asterisk	Any number (including zero); sometimes used as general wildcard
+	Plus	One or more of the preceding expression
{*N*}	Match exactly	Match exactly *N* times
{*N*,}	Match at least	Match at least *N* times
{*min,max*}	Specified range	Match between *min* and *max* times
Other		
|	Alternation	Matches either expression given
-	Dash	Indicates a range
(...)	Parentheses	Used to limit scope of alternation

Metacharacter	Name	Matches
\1, \2, ...	Backreference	Matches text previously matched within parentheses (e.g., first set, second set, etc.)
\b	Word boundary	Batches characters that typically mark the end of a word (e.g., space, period, etc.)
\B	Backslash	This is an alternative to using "\\" to match a backslash, used for readability
\w	Word character	This is used to match any "word" character (i.e., any letter, number, and the underscore character)
\W	Non-word character	This matches any character that isn't used in words (i.e., not a letter, number, or underscore)
\`	Start of buffer	Matches the start of a buffer sent to *grep*
\'	End of buffer	Matches the end of a buffer sent to *grep*

[a] From Jeffrey E.F. Friedl's *Mastering Regular Expressions* (O'Reilly), with some additions

The table references something known as the escape character. There are times when you will be required to search for a literal character that is usually used as a metacharacter. For example, suppose you are looking for amounts that contain the dollar sign within *price.list*:

```
grep '[1-9]$' price.list
```

As a result, the search will try to match the numbers at the end of the line. This is certainly something you do not want. By using the escape character, annotated by the backslash (\), you avoid such confusion:

```
grep '[1-9]\$' price.list
```

The metacharacter $ becomes a literal, and therefore is searched in *price.list* as a string.

For instance, take a text file (*price.list*) that has the following content:

```
123
123$
```

Using the two commands just shown yields the following
results:

```
$ grep '[1-9]\$' price.list
123$
$ grep '[1-9]$' price.list
123
```

In the first example, the command looked for the actual dollar-
sign character. In the second example, the dollar sign had its
special metacharacter's meaning and matched the end of line,
and so would match only those lines that ended in a number.
The meaning of these special characters needs to be kept in
mind because they can make a significant difference in how a
search is processed.

Here is a brief rundown of the regular expression metacharacters, along with some examples to make it clear how they are
used:

. *(any single character)*
    The "dot" character is one of the few types of wildcards
    available in regular expressions. This particular wildcard
    will match any single character. This is useful if a user
    wishes to craft a search pattern with some characters in
    the middle of it that are not known to the user. For in-
    stance, the following *grep* pattern would match "red",
    "rod", "red", "rzd", and so on:

    ```
    'r.d'
    ```

    This "dot" character can be used repeatedly at whatever
    interval is necessary to find the desired content.

[...] *(character class)*
    The "character class" tool is one of the more flexible tools,
    and it comes up again and again when using regular ex-
    pressions. There are two basic ways to use character
    classes: to specify a range and to specify a list of characters.
    An important point is that a character class will match
    only one character:

```
'[a-f]'
'[aeiou]'
```

The first pattern will look for any letter between "a" and "f". Ranges can be uppercase letters, lowercase letters, or numbers. A combination of ranges can also be used, for instance, [a-fA-F0-5]. The second example will search for any of the given characters, in this case vowels. A character class can also include a list of special characters, but they can't be used as a range.

[^...] *(negation)*

The "negation" character class allows a user to search for anything but a specific character or set of characters. For instance, a user who doesn't like even numbers could use the following search pattern:

```
'..[^24680]'
```

This will look for any three-character pattern that does not end in an even number. Any list or range of characters can be placed inside a negated character class.

\ *(escape)*

The "escape" is one of the metacharacters that can have multiple meanings depending on how it is used. When placed before another metacharacter, it signifies to treat that character as the literal symbol instead of its special meaning. (It also can be used in combination with other characters, such as b or ', to convey a special meaning. Those specific combinations are covered later.) Take the following two examples:

```
'.'
'\.'
```

The first example would match any single character and would return every piece of text in a file. The second example would only match the actual "period" character. The escape tells the regular expression to ignore the metacharacter's special meaning and process it normally.

^ (start of line)

When a carat is used outside of a character class, it no longer means negation; instead, it means the beginning of a line. If used by itself, it will match every single line on the screen because each line has a beginning. More useful is when a user wishes to match lines of text that begin with a certain pattern:

`'^red'`

This pattern would match all lines that begin with "red", not just the ones that contain the word "red". This is useful for structured communication or programming languages, for example, where lines may begin with specific strings that contain important information (such as `#DEFINE` in C). However, the meaning is lost if it is not at the beginning of a line.

$ (end of line)

As discussed earlier, the dollar sign character matches the end of a line. Used alone, it will match every line in a stream except the final line, which is terminated by an "end of file" character instead of an "end of line" character. This is useful for finding strings that have a desired meaning at the end of a line. For instance:

`'-$'`

would find all lines whose last character is a dash, as is typical for words that are hyphenated when they are too long to fit on one line. This expression would find only those lines with hyphenated words split between lines.

\< (start of word)

If a user wished to craft a search pattern that matches based on the start of a word and the pattern was likely to recur inside a word (but not at the beginning), this particular escape could be used. For instance, take the following example:

`'\<un'`

This pattern would match words starting with the prefix "un", such as "unimaginable," "undetected," or "undervalued." It would not match words such as "funding," "blunder," or "sun." It detects the beginning of a word by looking for a space or another "separation" that indicates the beginning of a new word (a period, comma, etc.).

\> *(end of word)*

Similar to the previous escape, this one will match at the end of a word. After the characters, it looks for a "separation" character that indicates the end of a word (a space, tab, period, comma, etc.). For example:

```
'ing\>'
```

would match words that end in "ing" (e.g., "spring"), not words that simply contain "ing" (e.g., "kingdom").

* *(general wildcard)*

The asterisk is probably by far the most-used metacharacter. It is a general wildcard classed as a quantifier that is specifically used for repetitious patterns. For some metacharacters, you can assign minimum and maximum boundaries that manipulate the quantity outputted from the pattern, but the asterisk does not place any limits or boundaries. There are no limits to how many spaces there can be before or after the character. Suppose a user wants to know whether a particular installer's different formats are described in a file. The results of this simple command:

```
'install.*file'
```

the results should output all the lines that contain "install" (with any amount of text in between) and then "file". It is necessary to use the period character; otherwise, it will match only "installfile" instead of iterations of "install" and "file" with characters in between.

- *(range)*

When used inside a bracketed character class, the dash character specifies a range of values instead of a raw list of values. When the dash is used outside of a bracketed character class, it is interpreted as the literal dash character, without its special value.

```
'[0-5]'
```

\# *(backreferences)*

Backreferences allow you to reuse a previously matched pattern to determine future matches. The format for a backreference is \ followed by the pattern number in the sequence (from left to right) that is being referenced. Backreferences are covered in more detail in the section "Advanced Tips and Tricks with grep" on page 57.

\b *(word boundary)*

The **\b** escape refers to any character that indicates a word has started or ended (similar to \> and \<, discussed earlier). In this case, it doesn't matter whether it is the beginning or end of the word; it simply looks for punctuation or spacing. This is particularly useful when you are searching for a string that can be a standalone word or a set of characters within another, unrelated word:

```
'\bheart\b'
```

This would match the exact word "heart" and nothing more (not "disheartening", not "hearts", etc.). If you are searching for a particular word, numerical value, or string and do not want to match when those words or values are part of another value, it is necessary to use either \b, \>, or \<.

\B *(backslash)*

The **\B** escape is a peculiar case because it isn't an escape itself, but rather an alias for another one. In this case, **\B** is identical to \\, namely, to interpret the slash character literally in a search pattern instead of with its special meaning. The purpose of this alias is to make a search pattern a little more readable and to avoid double-slashes, which could have ambiguous meaning in complicated expressions.

```
'c:\Bwindows'
```

This example would search for the string "c:\windows".

\w *and* \W *(word or non-word characters)*

The \w and \W escapes go hand in hand because their meanings are opposite. \w will match any "word" character and is equivalent to ``[a-zA-Z0-9_]``. The \W escape will match every other character (including non-printable ones) that does not fall into the "word character" category. This can be useful in parsing structured files where text is interposed with special characters (e.g., :, $, %, etc.).

\\` *(start of buffer)*

This escape, like the "start of line" escape, will match the start of a buffer as it is fed to whatever is processing the regular expression. Because *grep* works with lines, a buffer and a line tend to be synonymous (but not always). This escape is used in the same way as the "start of line" escape discussed earlier.

\\' *(end of buffer)*

This escape is similar to the "end of line" escape, except that it looks for the end of a buffer that is fed to whatever is processing the regular expression. In both cases of start and end of buffer escapes, their usage is extremely rare, and it is easier to simply use start and end of line instead.

The following is a list of metacharacters used in extended regular expressions:

? *(optional match)*

The use of the question mark has a different meaning than it does in typical filename wildcard usage (GLOB). In GLOB, ? means any single character. In regular expressions, it means that the preceding character (or string if placed after a subpattern) is an "optional" matching pattern. This allows for multiple match conditions with a single regular expression pattern. For instance:

```
'colors?'
```

would match both "color" and "colors". The "s" character is an optional match, so if it is not present, it does not cause a failing condition on the pattern.

+ *(repetitive match)*

The plus sign indicates that the regular expression is looking for a match of one or more of the previous character (or subpattern). For instance:

```
'150+'
```

would match 150 with any number of additional zeroes (e.g., 1500, 15000, 1500000, etc.).

{N} *(match exactly N times)*

Brackets, when placed after a character, indicate a specific number of repetitions to search for. For instance:

```
'150{3}\b'
```

would match 15 followed by 3 zeroes. So 1500 would not match, but 15000 would. Note the use of the \b "word boundary" escape. In this case, if the desired match is precisely "15000" and there is not a check for a word boundary "150000", "150002345" or "15000asdf" would match also because they all contain the desired search string of "15000".

{N,} *(match at least N times)*

Like the previous example, putting a number and a comma after it indicates the regular expression will search for at least N number of repetitions. For instance:

```
'150{3,}\b'
```

would match "15" followed by at least three zeroes, and so "15", "150", and "1500" would not match. Use the word boundary escape to avoid cases where a precise match of a specific number is desired. (e.g., "1500003456", "15000asdf", etc.). The use of \b clarifies the meaning.

{N,M} *(match between N and M times)*

If you wish to match some numbers between two values of repetitions, it is possible to specify both between the braces separated by a comma. For instance:

```
'150{2,3}\b'
```

would match "1500" and "15000" and nothing else.

| *(alternation)*

The "pipe" character specifies alternation inside a regular expression. Think of it as a way of giving the regular expression a choice of match conditions with a single expression. For example:

```
'apple|orange|banana|peach'
```

would match any of the strings given, regardless of whether the others are also within the scope of the search. In this case, if the text includes "apple" or "orange" or "banana" or "peach", it will match that content.

( ) *(subpattern)*

The last important feature of extended regular expressions is the ability to create subpatterns. This allows for regular expressions that repeat entire strings, use alternation on entire strings, to have backreferences work, and to make regular expressions more readable:

```
'(red|blue) plate'
'(150){3}'
```

The first example will match either "red plate" or "blue plate". Without the parentheses, the regular expression ''red|blue plate'' would match "red" (note the lack of the word "plate") or "blue plate". Parenthetical subpatterns help limit the scope of alternation.

In the second example, the regular expression will match on "150150150". Without parentheses, it would match "15000". Parentheses make it possible to match on repetition of entire strings instead of single characters.

Metacharacters generally are universal between the different *grep* commands, such as *egrep*, *fgrep*, and *grep* -P. However, there are instances in which a character carries a different connotation. Any differences will be discussed within the section pertaining to that command.

POSIX Character Classes

Additionally, regular expressions come with a set of POSIX character definitions that create shortcuts to find certain classes of characters. Table 2 shows a list of these shortcuts and what they signify. POSIX is basically a set of standards created by the Institute of Electrical and Electronics Engineers (IEEE) to describe how Unix-style operating systems should behave. It is very old, but much of its content is still used. Among other things, POSIX has definitions on how regular expressions should work with shell utilities such as *grep*.

Table 2. POSIX character definitions

POSIX definition	Contents of character definition
[:alpha:]	Any alphabetical character, regardless of case
[:digit:]	Any numerical character
[:alnum:]	Any alphabetical or numerical character
[:blank:]	Space or tab characters
[:xdigit:]	Hexadecimal characters; any number or A–F or a–f
[:punct:]	Any punctuation symbol
[:print:]	Any printable character (not control characters)
[:space:]	Any whitespace character
[:graph:]	Exclude whitespace characters
[:upper:]	Any uppercase letter
[:lower:]	Any lowercase letter
[:cntrl:]	Control characters

Many of these POSIX definitions are more readable equivalents of character classes. For instance, [:upper:] can be also written as [A-Z] and uses less characters to do so. There aren't good character class equivalents for some other classes, such as [:cntrl:]. To use these in a regular expression, simply place them the same way you would place a character class. It is important to note that one placement of these POSIX character definitions will match only one single character. To match repetitions of character classes, you would have to repeat the definition. For instance:

```
'[:digit:]'
'[:digit:][:digit:][:digit:]'
'[:digit:]{3}'
```

In the first example, any single numerical character will be matched. In the second example, only three-digit numbers (or longer) will be matched. The third example is a cleaner, shorter way of writing the second example. Many regular expressions enthusiasts try to accomplish as much as possible with as few keystrokes as possible. Show them the second example, and they may cringe. The third example is a more efficient way of accomplishing the same thing.

Crafting a Regular Expression

Like algebra, *grep* has rules of precedence for processing. Repetition is processed before concatenation. Concatenation is processed before alternation. Strings are concatenated by simply being next to each other inside the regular expression—there is no special character to signify concatenation.

For instance, take the following regular expression:

```
'pat{2}ern|red'
```

In this example, the repetition is processed first, yielding two "t"s. Then, the strings are concatenated, producing "pattern" on one side of the pipe and "red" on the other. Next, the alternation is processed, creating a regular expression that will search for "pattern" or "red". However, what if you wanted to search for "patpatern" and "red" or "pattern" or "pattred"?

In this case, just like in algebra, parentheses will "override" the rules of precedence. For example:

```
2 + 3 / 5
(2 + 3) / 5
```

These two mathematical equations yield different results because of the parentheses. The concept is the same here:

```
'(pat){2}ern|red'
'pat{2}(ern|red)'
```

The first example will concatenate "pat" first and then repeat it twice, yielding "patpattern" and "red" as the search strings. The second example will process the alternation subpattern first, so the regular expression will search for "pattern" and "pattred". Using parentheses can help you fine-tune your regular expression to match specific content based on how you construct it. Even if the rules of precedence don't need to be overruled for a particular regular expression, sometimes it makes sense to use parentheses for enhanced readability.

A regular expression can continue as long as the single quote is not closed. For instance:

```
$ grep 'patt
> ern' filename
```

Here the single quote was not ended before the user pressed Return right after the second "t" (no space was pressed). The next line shows a > prompt, which indicates it is still waiting for the string to be completed before it processes the command. As long as you keep pressing Return, it will keep giving you the prompt until you either press Ctrl-C to break or close the quote, at which point it will process the command. This allows for long regular expressions to be typed in on the command line (or a shell script) without cramming them all on one line, potentially making them less than readable.

In this case, the regular expression searches for the word "pattern". The command ignores returns and does not input those into the regular expression itself, so it is possible to hit Enter in the middle of a word and pick up right where you left off.

Concern for readability is important because "space" keys aren't easily visible, which makes this example a great contender for subpatterns, to help make the regular expression more understandable.

It is also possible to use several different groupings of strings with their own quotation marks. For instance:

```
'patt''ern'
```

would search for the word "pattern", just as if it were typed with the expected regular expression of `''pattern''`. This example isn't a very practical one, and there is no compelling reason ever to do that with just text. However, when combining different quotation types, this technique makes it possible to take advantage of each quotation type to produce a regular expression using environment variables and/or output from commands. For example:

```
$ echo $HOME
/home/bambenek
$ whoami
bambenek
```

shows that the environment variable $HOME is set to */home/ bambenek* and that the output of the command *whoami* is "bambenek". So, the following regular expression:

```
'username:'`whoami`' and home directory
is '"$HOME"
```

would match on the string "username:bambenek and home directory is /home/bambenek" by inserting in the output from the *whoami* command and the setting for the environment variable $HOME. This is a quick overview of regular expressions and how they can be used. There are entire books devoted to the complexities of regular expressions, but this primer is enough to get you started on what you need to know in order to use the *grep* command.

grep Basics

There are two ways to employ *grep*. The first examines files as follows:

```
grep regexp filename
```

grep searches for the designated **regexp** in the given file (**filename**). The second method of employing *grep* is when it examines "standard input." For example:

```
cat filename | grep regexp
```

In this case, the *cat* command will display the contents of a file. The output of this command is "piped" into the *grep* command, which will then display only those lines that contain the given regexp. The two commands just shown have identical results because the *cat* command simply passes the file unchanged, but the second form is valuable for "grepping" other commands that alter their input.

When *grep* is called without a filename argument and without being passed any input, it will let you type in text and will repeat it once it gets a line that contains the regexp. To exit, press Ctrl-D.

At times, the output is remarkably large and hard to scroll through in a terminal. This is usually the case with large files that tend to have repetitious phrases, such as an error log. In these cases, piping the output to the *more* or *less* commands will "paginate" it so that only one screen of text is shown at a time:

```
grep regexp filename | more
```

Another option to make the output easier to look at is to redirect the results into a new file and then open the output file in a text editor at a later time:

```
grep regexp filename > newfilename
```

Also, it may be advantageous to look for lines that contain several patterns instead of just one. In the following example, the text file *editinginfo* contains a date, a username, and the file that was edited by that user on the given date. If an administrator was interested in just the files edited by "Smith", he would type the following:

```
cat editinginfo | grep Smith
```

The output would look like:

```
May 20, 2008       Smith       hi.txt
June 21, 2008      Smith       world.txt
     .
     .
```

An administrator may wish to match multiple patterns, which can be accomplished by "chaining" *grep* commands together. We are now familiar with the `cat filename | grep regexp` command and what it does. By piping the second *grep*, along with any number of piped *grep* commands, you create a very refined search:

```
cat filename | grep regexp | grep regexp2
```

In this case, the command looks for lines in *filename* that have both *regexp* and *regexp2*. More specifically, *grep* will search for *regexp2* in the results of the *grep* search for *regexp*. Using the previous example, if an administrator wanted to see every date that Smith edited any file except *hi.txt*, he could issue the following command:

```
cat editinginfo | grep Smith | grep -v hi.txt
```

The following output would result:

```
June 21, 2008       Smith    world.txt
```

It is important to note that "chaining" *grep* commands is inefficient most of the time. Often, a regular expression can be crafted to combine several conditions into a single search.

For instance, instead of the previous example, which combines three different commands, the same could be accomplished with:

```
grep Smith | grep -v hi.txt
```

Using the pipe character will run one command and give the results of that command to the next command in the sequence.

In this case, *grep* searches for lines with "Smith" in them and sends those results to the next *grep* command, which excludes lines that have "hi.txt". When a search can be accomplished using fewer commands or with fewer decisions having to be made, the more efficiently it will behave. For small files, performance isn't an issue, but when searching through gigabyte-sized logfiles, performance can be an important consideration.

There is a case to be made for piping commands when you wish to search through content that is continually streaming. For instance, if you want to monitor a logfile in real-time for specified content, she could use the following command:

```
tail -f /var/log/messages | grep WARNING
```

This command would open up the last 10 lines of the */var/log/messages* files (usually the main system logfile on a Linux system), but keep the file open and print all content placed into the file as long as it is running (the -f option to *tail* is often called "follow"). So the command just shown would look for any entry that has the string "WARNING" in it, display it to the console, and disregard all other messages.

As an important note, *grep* will search through a line and once it sees a newline, it will restart the entire search on the next line. This means that if you are searching for a sentence with *grep*, there is a very real possibility that a newline character in the middle of the sentence in the file will prevent you from finding that sentence directly. Even specifying the newline character in the search pattern will not alleviate this problem. Some text editors and productivity applications simply wrap words on lines without placing a newline character, so searching is not pointless in these cases, but it is an important limitation to keep in mind.

To get details about the regular expression implementation on your specific machine, check the `regex` and `re_format` manpages. It is important to note, however, that not all the functions and abilities of regular expressions are built-in to *grep*. For instance, search and replace is not available. More importantly, there are some useful escape characters that seem to be missing by default.

For instance, \d is an escape sequence to match any numeric character (0 through 9) in some regular expressions. However, this does not seem to be available with *grep* under standard distribution and compile options (with the exception of Perl-style *grep*, to be covered later). This guide attempts to cover what is available by default in a standard installation and attempts to be the authoritative resource on the abilities and limits of *grep*.

The *grep* program is actually a package of four different pattern-matching programs that use different regular-expression models. Each pattern-matching system has its strengths and weaknesses, and each will be discussed in detail in the following sections. We'll start with the original model, which we'll call basic *grep*.

Basic Regular Expressions (grep or grep -G)

This section focuses on basic *grep*. Most of the flags for basic *grep* apply equally to the other versions, which we'll discuss later.

Basic *grep*, or *grep -G*, is the default pattern matching type that is used when calling *grep*. *grep* interprets the given set of patterns as a basic regular expression when it executes the command. This is the default *grep* program that is called, so the -G option is almost always redundant.

Like any command, *grep* comes with a handful of options that control both the matches found and the way *grep* displays the results. The GNU version of *grep* offers most of the options listed in the following subsections.

Match Control

-e *pattern*, **--regexp=***pattern*

```
grep -e -style doc.txt
```

Ensures that *grep* recognizes the pattern as the regular expression argument. Useful if the regular expression begins with a hyphen, which makes it look like an option. In this case, *grep* will look for lines that match "-style".

-f *file*, **--file=***file*

```
grep -f pattern.txt searchhere.txt
```

Takes patterns from *file*. This option allows you to input all the patterns you want to match into a file, called *pattern.txt* here. Then, *grep* searches for all the patterns from *pattern.txt* in the designated file *searchhere.txt*. The patterns are additive; that is, *grep* returns every line that matches any pattern. The pattern file must list one pattern per line. If *pattern.txt* is empty, nothing will match.

-i, **--ignore-case**

```
grep -i 'help' me.txt
```

Ignores capitalization in the given regular expressions, either via the command line or in a file of regular expressions specified by the **-f** option. The example here would search the file *me.txt* for a string "help" with any iteration of lower- and uppercase letters in the word ("HELP", "HelP", etc.). A similar but obsolete synonym to this option is **-y**.

-v, **--invert-match**

```
grep -v oranges filename
```

Returns lines that do *not* match, instead of lines that do. In this case, the output would be every line in *filename* that does not contain the pattern "oranges".

`-w, --word-regexp`

```
grep -w 'xyz' filename
```

Matches only when the input text consists of full words. In this example, it is not enough for a line to contain the three letters "xyz" in a row; there must actually be spaces or punctuation around them. Letters, digits, and the underscore character are all considered part of a word; any other character is considered a word boundary, as are the start and end of the line. This is the equivalent of putting \b at the beginning and end of the regular expression.

`-x, --line-regexp`

```
grep -x 'Hello, world!' filename
```

Like -w, but must match an entire line. This example matches only lines that consist entirely of "Hello, world!". Lines that have additional content will not be matched. This can be useful for parsing logfiles for specific content that might include cases you are not interested in seeing.

General Output Control

`-c, --count`

```
grep -c contact.html access.log
```

Instead of the normal output, you receive just a count of how many lines matched in each input file. In the example here, *grep* will simply return the number of times the *contact.html* file was accessed through a web server's access log.

```
grep -c -v contact.html access.log
```

This example returns a count of all the lines that do *not* match the given string. In this case, it would be every time someone accessed a file that wasn't *contact.html* on the web server.

`--color[=WHEN]`, `--colour[=WHEN]`

>   grep -color[=auto] *regexp filename*

Assuming the terminal can support color, *grep* will colorize the pattern in the output. This is done by surrounding the matched (nonempty) string, matching lines, context lines, filenames, line numbers, byte offsets, and separators with escape sequences that the terminal recognizes as color markers. Color is defined by the environment variable `GREP_COLORS` (discussed later). `WHEN` has three options: `never`, `always`, and `auto`.

`-l`, `--files-with-matches`

>   grep -l "ERROR:" *.log

Instead of normal output, prints just the names of input files containing the pattern. As with `-L`, the search stops on the first match. If an administrator is simply interested in the filenames that contain a pattern without seeing all the matching lines, this option performs that function. This can make *grep* more efficient by stopping the search as soon as it finds a matching pattern instead of continuing to search an entire file. This is often referred to as "lazy matching."

`-L`, `--files-without-match`

>   grep -L 'ERROR:' *.log

Instead of normal output, prints just the names of input files that contain no matches. For instance, the example prints all the logfiles that contain no reports of errors. This is an efficient use of *grep* because it stops searching each file once it finds any match, instead of continuing to search the entire file for multiple matches.

`-m` *NUM*, `--max-count=`*NUM*

>   grep -m 10 'ERROR:' *.log

This option tells *grep* to stop reading a file after *NUM* lines are matched (in this example, only 10 lines that contain "ERROR:"). This is useful for reading large files where repetition is likely, such as logfiles. If you simply want to see whether strings are present without flooding the terminal, use this option. This helps to distinguish between pervasive and intermittent errors, as in the example here.

`-o, --only-matching`

```
grep -o pattern filename
```

Prints only the text that matches, instead of the whole line of input. This is particularly useful when implementing *grep* to examine a disk partition or a binary file for the presence of multiple patterns. This would output the pattern that was matched without the content that would cause problems for the terminal.

`-q, --quiet, --silent`

```
grep -q pattern filename
```

Suppresses output. The command still conveys useful information because the *grep* command's exit status (0 for success if a match is found, 1 for no match found, 2 if the program cannot run because of an error) can be checked. The option is used in scripts to determine the presence of a pattern in a file without displaying unnecessary output.

`-s, --no-messages`

```
grep -s pattern filename
```

Silently discards any error messages resulting from nonexistent files or permission errors. This is helpful for scripts that search an entire filesystem without root permissions, and thus will likely encounter permissions errors that may be undesirable. On the other side, it also will suppress useful diagnostic information, which could mean that problems may not be discovered.

Output Line Prefix Control

`-b, --byte-offset`

```
grep -b pattern filename
```

Displays the byte offset of each matching text instead of the line number. The first byte in the file is byte 0, and invisible line-terminating characters (the newline in Unix) are counted. Because entire lines are printed by default, the number displayed is the byte offset of the start of the line. This is particularly useful for binary file analysis, constructing (or reverse-engineering) patches, or other tasks where line numbers are meaningless.

```
grep -b -o pattern filename
```

A -o option prints the offset along with the matched pattern itself and not the whole matched line containing the pattern. This causes *grep* to print the byte offset of the start of the matched string instead of the matched line.

-H, --with-filename

```
grep -H pattern filename
```

Includes the name of the file before each line printed, and is the default when more than one file is input to the search. This is useful when searching only one file and you want the filename to be contained in the output. Note that this uses the relative (not absolute) paths and filenames.

-h, --no-filename

```
grep -h pattern *
```

The opposite of -H. When more than one file is involved, it suppresses printing the filename before each output. It is the default when only one file or standard input is involved. This is useful for suppressing filenames when searching entire directories.

--label=*LABEL*

```
gzip -cd file.gz | grep --label=LABEL pattern
```

When the input is taken from standard input (for instance, when the output of another file is redirected into *grep*), the --label option will prefix the line with LABEL. In this example, the *gzip* command displays the contents of the uncompressed file inside *file.gz* and then passes that to *grep*.

`-n, --line-number`

> `grep -n` *pattern filename*

Includes the line number of each line displayed, where the first line of the file is 1. This can be useful in code debugging, allowing you to go into the file and specify a particular line number to start editing.

`-T, --initial-tab`

> `grep -T` *pattern filename*

Inserts a tab before each matching line, putting the tab between the information generated by *grep* and the matching lines. This option is useful for clarifying the layout. For instance, it can separate line numbers, byte offsets, labels, etc., from the matching text.

`-u, --unix-byte-offsets`

> `grep -u -b` *pattern filename*

This option only works under the MS-DOS and Microsoft Windows platforms and needs to be invoked with `-b`. This option will compute the byte-offset as if it were running under a Unix system and strip out carriage return characters.

`-Z, --null`

> `grep -Z` *pattern filename*

Prints an ASCII NUL (a zero byte) after each filename. This is useful when processing filenames that may contain special characters (such as carriage returns).

Context Line Control

`-A NUM, --after-context=NUM`

> `grep -A 3 Copyright` *filename*

Offers a context for matching lines by printing the *NUM* lines that follow each match. A group separator (--) is placed between each set of matches. In this case, it will print the next three lines after the matching line. This is useful when searching through source code, for instance. The example here will print three lines after any line that contains "Copyright", which is typically at the top of source code files.

`-B` *NUM*, `--before-context=`*NUM*

```
grep -B 3 Copyright filename
```

Same concept as the `-A` *NUM* option, except that it prints the lines *before* the match instead of after it. In this case, it will print the three lines before the matching line. This is useful when searching through source code, for instance. The example here will print three lines before any line that contains "Copyright", which is typically at the top of source code files.

`-C` *NUM*, `-`*NUM*, `--context=`*NUM*

```
grep -C 3 Copyright filename
```

The `-C` *NUM* option operates as if the user entered both the `-A` *NUM* and `-B` *NUM* options. It will display *NUM* lines before and after the match. A group separator (--) is placed between each set of matches. In this case, three lines above and below the matching line will be printed. Again, this is useful when searching through source code, for instance. The example here will print three lines before and after any line that contains "Copyright", which is typically at the top of source code files.

File and Directory Selection

`-a`, `--text`

```
grep -a pattern filename
```

Equivalent to the `--binary-files=text` option, allowing a binary file to be processed as if it were a text file.

--binary-files=*TYPE*

```
grep --binary-files=TYPE pattern filename
```

TYPE can be either `binary`, `without-match`, or `text`. When *grep* first examines a file, it determines whether the file is a "binary" file (a file primarily composed of non-human-readable text) and changes its output accordingly. By default, a match in a binary file causes *grep* to display simply the message "Binary file *somefile.bin* matches." The default behavior can also be specified with the `--binary-files=binary` option.

When *TYPE* is `without-match`, *grep* does not search the binary file and proceeds as if it had no matches (equivalent to the `-l` option). When *TYPE* is `text`, the binary file is processed like text (equivalent to the `-a` option). When *TYPE* is `without-match`, *grep* will simply skip those files and not search through them. Sometimes `--binary-files=text` outputs binary garbage and the terminal may interpret some of that garbage as commands, which in turn can render the terminal unreadable until reset. To recover from this, use the commands *tput init* and *tput reset*.

-D *ACTION*, --devices=*ACTION*

```
grep -D read 123-45-6789 /dev/hda1
```

If the input file is a special file, such as a FIFO or a socket, this flag tells *grep* how to proceed. By default, *grep* will process these files as if they were normal files on a system. If *ACTION* is set to `skip`, *grep* will silently ignore them. The example will search an entire disk partition for the fake Social Security number shown. When *ACTION* is set to `read`, *grep* will read through the device as if it were a normal file.

-d *ACTION*, --directories=*ACTION*

```
grep -d ACTION pattern path
```

This flag tells *grep* how to process directories submitted as input files. When *ACTION* is `read`, this reads the directory as if it were a file. `recurse` searches the files within that directory (same as the -R option), and skip skips the directory without searching it.

--exclude=_GLOB_

> grep --exclude=_PATTERN_ _path_

Refines the list of input files by telling *grep* to ignore files whose names match the specified pattern. _PATTERN_ can be an entire filename or can contain the typical "file-globbing" wildcards the shell uses when matching files (*, ? and []). For instance, --exclude=*.exe will skip all files ending in _.exe_.

--exclude-from=_FILE_

> grep --exclude-from=_FILE_ _path_

Similar to the --exclude option, except that it takes a list of patterns from a specified filename, which lists each pattern on a separate line. *grep* will ignore all files that match any lines in the list of patterns given.

--exclude-dir=_DIR_

> grep --exclude-dir=DIR _pattern_ _path_

Any directories in the path matching the pattern _DIR_ will be excluded from recursive searches. In this case, the actual directory name (relative name or absolute path name) has to be included to be ignored. This option also must be used with the -r option or the -d recurse option in order to be relevant.

-l

> grep -l _pattern_ _filename_

Same as the --binary-files=without-match option. When *grep* finds a binary file, it will assume there is no match in the file.

--include=_GLOB_

> grep --include=*.log _pattern_ _filename_

Limits searches to input files whose names match the given pattern (in this case, files ending in _.log_). This option is particularly useful when searching directories using the -R option. Files not matching the given pattern will be ignored. An entire filename can be specified, or can contain the typical "file-globbing" wildcards the shell uses when matching files (*, ? and []).

`-R, -r, --recursive`

```
grep -R pattern path
grep -r pattern path
```

Searches all files underneath each directory submitted as an input file to *grep*.

Other Options

`--line-buffered`

```
grep --line-buffered pattern filename
```

Uses line buffering for the output. Line buffering output usually leads to a decrease in performance. The default behavior of *grep* is to use unbuffered output. This is generally a matter of preference.

`--mmap`

```
grep --mmap pattern filename
```

Uses the `mmap()` function instead of the `read()` function to process data. This can lead to a performance improvement but may cause errors if there is an I/O problem or the file shrinks while being searched.

`-U, --binary`

```
grep -U pattern filename
```

An MS-DOS/Windows-specific option that causes *grep* to treat all files as binary. Normally, *grep* would strip out carriage returns before doing pattern matching; this option overrides that behavior. This does, however, require you to be more thoughtful when writing patterns. For instance, if content in a file contains the pattern but has a newline character in the middle, a search for that pattern will not find the content.

-V, --version

Simply outputs the version information about *grep* and then exits.

-z, --null-data

```
grep -z pattern
```

Input lines are treated as though each one ends with a zero byte, or the ASCII NUL character, instead of a newline. Similar to the -Z or --null options, except this option works with input, not output.

One final limitation of basic *grep*: the "extended" regular expressions metacharacters—?, +, {, }, |, (, and)—do not work with basic *grep*. The functions provided by those characters exist if you preface them with an escape. More on that in the next section.

Extended Regular Expressions (egrep or grep -E)

grep -E and *egrep* are the same exact command. The commands search files for patterns that have been interpreted as extended regular expressions. An extended regular expression goes beyond just using the previously mentioned options; it uses additional metacharacters to create more complex and powerful search strings. As far as command-line options, *grep -E* and *grep* take the same ones—the only differences are in how they process the search pattern:

?

? in an expression carries the meaning of *optional*. Any character preceding the question mark may or may not appear in the target string. For example, say you are looking for the word "behavior", which can also be written as "behaviour". Instead of using the *or* (|) option, you can use the command:

```
egrep 'behaviou?r' filename
```

As a result, the search is successful for both "behavior" and "behaviour" because it will treat the presence or absence of the letter "u" the same way.

+

The plus sign will look at the previous character and allow an unlimited amount of repetitions when it looks for matching strings. For instance, the following command would match both "pattern1" and "pattern11111", but would not match "pattern":

```
egrep 'pattern1+' filename
```

{*n*,*m*}

The braces are used to determine how many times a pattern needs to be repeated before a match occurs. For instance, instead of searching for "patternnnn", you could enter the following command:

```
egrep 'pattern{4}' filename
```

This will match any string that contains "patternnnn" without going through the trouble of typing out repeated strings. In order to match at least four repetitions, you would use the following command:

```
egrep 'pattern{4,}' filename
```

On the other hand, look at the following example:

```
egrep 'pattern{,4}' filename
```

Despite the fact that it would fit in with the conventions already used, this is *not* valid. The command just shown would result in no matches because the ability to have "no more than *X*" matches is not available.

To match between four and six repetitions, use the following:

```
egrep 'pattern{4,6}' filename
```

|

Used in a regular expression, this character signifies "or."
As a result, pipe (|) allows you to combine several patterns
into one expression. For example, suppose you need to
find either of two names in file. You could issue the following command:

```
egrep 'name1|name2' filename
```

It would match on lines containing either "name1" or
"name2".

( )

Parentheses can be used to "group" particular strings of
text for the purposes of backreferences, alternation, or
simply readability. Additionally, the use of parentheses
can help resolve any ambiguity in precisely what the user
wants the search pattern to do. Patterns placed inside parentheses are often called subpatterns.

Also parentheses put limits on pipe (|). This allows the
user to more tightly define which strings are part of or in
scope of the "or" operation. For instance, to search for
lines that contain either "pattern" or "pattarn", you would
use the following command:

```
egrep 'patt(a|e)rn' filename
```

Without the parentheses, the search pattern would be
patta|ern, which would match if the string "patta" or
"ern" is found, a very different outcome than the inten-
tion.

In basic regular expressions, the backslash (\) negates the
metacharacter's behavior and forces the search to match the
character in a literal sense. The same happens in *egrep*, but
there is an exception. The metacharacter { is not supported by
the traditional *egrep*. Although some versions interpret \{ literally, it should be avoided in *egrep* patterns. Instead, [{]
should be used to match the character without invoking the
special meaning.

It is not precisely true that basic *grep* does not have these metacharacters as well. It does, but they cannot be used directly. Each of the special metacharacters in extended regular expressions needs to be prefaced by an escape to draw out its special meaning. Note that this is the reverse of normal escaping behavior, which usually strips special meaning.

Table 3 illustrates how to use the extended regular expressions metacharacters with basic *grep*.

Table 3. Basic versus extended regular expressions comparison

Basic regular expressions	Extended regular expressions
`'\(red\)'`	`'(red)'`
`'a\{1,3\}'`	`'a{1,3}'`
`'behaviou\?r'`	`'behaviou?r'`
`'pattern\+'`	`'pattern+'`

From Table 3, you get the idea why people would prefer to just use extended *grep* when they want to use extended regular expressions. Convenience aside, it is also easy to forget to place a necessary escape in basic regular expressions, which would cause the pattern to silently not return any matches. An ideal regular expression should be clear and use as few characters as possible.

Fixed Strings (fgrep or grep -F)

In the following section, we discuss *grep -F*, or *fgrep*. *fgrep* is known as fixed string or fast *grep*. It is known as "fast grep" because of the great performance it has compared to *grep* and *egrep*. It accomplishes this by dropping regular expressions altogether and looking for a defined string pattern. It is useful for searching for specific static content in a precise manner, similar to the way Google operates.

The command to evoke *fgrep* is:

```
fgrep string_pattern filename
```

By design, *fgrep* was intended to operate fast and free of inten-
sive functions; as a result, it can take a more limited set of
command-line options. The most common ones are:

-b

```
fgrep -b string_pattern filename
```

Shows the block number where the **string_pattern** was
found. Because entire lines are printed by default, the byte
number displayed is the byte offset of the start of the line.

-c

```
fgrep -c string_pattern filename
```

This counts the number of lines that contain one or more
instances of the **string_pattern**.

-e, -string

```
fgrep -e string_pattern filename
```

Used for the search of more than one pattern or when the
string_pattern begins with hyphen. Though you can use
a newline character to specify more than one string, instead you could use multiple -e options, which is useful
in scripting:

```
fgrep -e string_pattern1
-e string_pattern2 filename
```

-f file

```
fgrep -f newfile string_pattern filename
```

Outputs the results of the search into a new file instead of
printing directly to the terminal. This is unlike the behavior of the -f option in grep; there it specifies a search pattern input file.

-h

```
fgrep -h string_pattern filename
```

When the search is done in more than one file, using -h
stops *fgrep* from displaying *filenames* before the matched
output.

-i

```
fgrep -i string_pattern filename
```

The -i option tells *fgrep* to ignore capitalization contained in the *string_pattern* when matching the pattern.

-l

```
fgrep -l string_pattern filename
```

Displays the files containing the *string_pattern* but not the matching lines themselves.

-n

```
fgrep -n string_pattern filename
```

Prints out the line number before the line that matches the given *string_pattern*.

-v

```
fgrep -v string_pattern filename
```

Matches any lines that do not contain the given *string_pattern*.

-x

```
fgrep -x string_pattern filename
```

Prints out the lines that match the *string_pattern* in their entirety. This is the default behavior of *fgrep*, so usually it does not need to be specified.

Perl-Style Regular Expressions (grep -P)

Perl-style regular expressions use the Perl-Compatible Regular Expressions (PCRE) library to interpret the pattern and perform searches. As the name implies, this style uses Perl's implementation of regular expressions. Perl has an advantage because the language was optimized for text searching and manipulation. As a result, PCRE can be more efficient and far more function-rich for finding content. The consequence is that it can be horribly messy and complex. To put it another way, using PCRE to find information is like using a weed whacker on yourself to do brain surgery: it gets the job done with minimum of effort, but it is an awful mess.

The specific search features and options with PCRE are not dependent upon *grep* itself, but use the libpcre library and the underlying version of Perl. This means that it can be highly variable between machines and operating systems. Usually the **pcrepattern** or **pcre** manpages will provide machine-specific information on the options that are available on your machine. What follows is a general set of PCRE search functions that should be available on most machines.

Also note that Perl-style regular expressions may or may not be present by default on your operating system. Fedora and Red Hat–based systems tend to include them (assuming you install the PCRE library), but Debian, for instance, does not enable Perl-style regular expressions by default in their *grep* package. Instead, they ship a *pcregrep* program, which provides very similar functionality to *grep -P*. Individuals can, of course, compile their own *grep* binary that does include PCRE support should they be so inclined.

To test whether Perl-style regular expression support is built-in to your version of *grep*, run the following command (or something like it):

```
$ grep -P test /bin/ls
grep: The -P option is not supported
```

This usually means that when *grep* was built it could not find the libpcre library or that it was intentionally disabled with the **--disable-perl-regexp** configuration option when it was compiled. The solution is to either install *libpcre* and recompile *grep* or find an applicable package for your operating system.

The general form of using Perl-style *grep* is:

```
grep -P options pattern file
```

It is important to note that, unlike *grep -F* and *grep -E*, there is no "*pgrep*" command. The *pgrep* command is used to search for running processes on a machine. All the same command-line options that are present for *grep* will work with *grep -P*; the only difference is how the pattern is processed. PCRE provides additional metacharacters and character classes that can be used enhance search functionality. Other than the additional metacharacters and classes, the pattern is constructed in the same way as a typical regular expression.

This section covers only four aspects of PCRE options: character types, octal searching, character properties, and PCRE options.

Character Types

Although there is some overlap here with standard *grep*, PCRE comes with its own set of escapes that provide a more robust set of matching. Table 4 contains the list of escapes available under PCRE.

Table 4. PCRE-specific escapes

\a	Matches the "alarm" character (HEX 07)
\c*X*	Matches Ctrl-*X*, where *X* is any letter
\e	Matches escape character (HEX 1B)
\f	Matches form feed character (HEX 0C)
\n	Matches newline character (HEX 0A)
\r	Matches carriage return (HEX 0D)
\t	Matches tab character (HEX 09)
\d	Any decimal digit
\D	Any non-decimal character
\s	Any whitespace character
\S	Any non-whitespace character
\w	Any "word" character
\W	Any "non-word" character

\b	Matches when at word boundary
\B	Matches when not at word boundary
\A	Matches when at start of subject
\Z	Matches when at end of subject or before newline
\z	Matches when at end of subject
\G	Matches at first matching position

Octal Searching

To search for octal charters, use the / metacharacter followed by the octal number of the metacharacter. For instance, to search for "space", use /40 or /040. However, this is one of the areas where PCRE can be ambiguous if you aren't careful. The / metacharacter can also be used for backreference (a reference to a previous pattern given to PCRE).

For instance, /1 is a backreference to the first pattern in a list, not octal character 1. To be free of ambiguity, the easiest way is to specify the octal character as a three-digit number. Up to 777 is permitted in UTF-8 mode. All single-digit numbers given after the slash are interpreted as a backreference, and if there have been more than *XX* patterns, then *XX* is interpreted as a backreference as well.

Additionally, PCRE can search from a character in hex format or a string of characters represented in hex format. \x0b will search for the hex character 0b, for example. To search for a hex string, simply use \x{0b0b....}, where the string is contained within the braces.

Character Properties

Additionally, PCRE comes with a set of functions that will search for characters based on their property. This comes in two particular flavors, language and character type. To use this, the \p or \P sequence is used. \p searches if a given property is present, whereas \P matches any character where it is not present.

To search for the presence (or absence) of characters that belong to a certain language, for example, you would use \p{Greek} to find Greek characters. \P{Greek}, on the other hand, would match any character that is not part of the Greek character set. For a complete list of languages available, consult the manpage for the particular *pcrepattern* implementation on your system.

The other set of properties refers to the attributes of a given character (uppercase, punctuation, etc.). The capital letter represents the major grouping of characters, and the small letter refers to the subgroup. If only the capital letter is specified (e.g., /p{L}), all subgroups are matched. Table 5 shows the complete list of property codes.

Table 5. PCRE character properties

C	Other	No	Other number
Cc	Control	P	Punctuation
Cf	Format	Pc	Connector punctuation
Cn	Unassigned	Pd	Dash punctuation
Co	Private use	Pe	Close punctuation
Cs	Surrogate	Pf	Final punctuation
L	Letter	Pi	Initial punctuation
Ll	Lowercase	Po	Other punctuation
Lm	Modifier	Ps	Open punctuation
Lo	Other letter	S	Symbol
Lt	Title case	Sc	Currency symbol
Lu	Uppercase	Sk	Modifier symbol
M	Mark	Sm	Mathematical symbol
Mc	Spacing mark	So	Other symbol
Me	Enclosing mark	Z	Separator
Mn	Non-spacing mark	Zl	Line separator

N	Number	Zp	Paragraph separator
Nd	Decimal	Zs	Space separator
Nl	Letter number		

These properties allows for creating more robust patterns with fewer characters based on a large number of properties. One important note, however: if *pcre* is compiled by hand, the `--enable-unicode-properties` configuration option must be used to compile in support for these options. Some *libpcre* packages (i.e., Fedora or Debian packages) have this built-in (especially internationally minded ones), but others do not. To check whether support is built-in to *pcre*, run the following (or something like it):

```
$ grep -P '\p{Cc}' /bin/ls
grep: support for \P, \p, and \X has not been compiled
```

That error message about support being compiled in has to do with *pcre* and not *grep*, which is not exactly intuitive. The solution is to either find a better package or compile your own with the correct options.

PCRE Options

Finally, there are four different options that can alter the way PCRE looks for text: PCRE_CASELESS (i), PCRE_MULTILINE (m), PCRE_DOTALL (s), and PCRE_EXTENDED (x). PCRE_CASELESS will match patterns regardless of differences in capitalization. By default, PCRE treats a line of text as one line, even if several \n characters are present. PCRE_MULTILINE will allow for treating those \n characters as lines, so if $ or ^ is used, it will search lines based on the presence of \n and actual hard lines in the search string.

PCRE_DOTALL causes PCRE to interpret the . (dot) metacharacter to include newlines when it does "wildcard" matching. PCRE_EXTENDED is useful for including comments (placed within unescaped # characters) in complicated search strings.

To enable these options, place the given option letter inside parentheses with a beginning question mark. For instance, to craft a pattern that will search for the word "copyright" in a caseless format, you would use the following pattern:

```
'(?i)copyright'
```

Any combination of letters can be used inside the parentheses. These options can be placed so that they operate on only part of the search string: simply place them at the beginning of the part of the string where the option should take effect. To negate an option, preface the letter with a - (hyphen). For example:

```
'Copy(?i)righ(?-i)t'
```

This would match "CopyRIGHt", "CopyrIgHt", and "Copyright", but it would not match "COPYright" or "CopyrighT".

```
'(?imsx)copy(?-sx)right'
```

This would set all the PCRE options we've discussed, but once it reaches the "r" character, `PCRE_DOTALL` and `PCRE_EXTENDED` would be turned off.

If using Perl-based regular expressions seems complicated, that's because it is. There is far more to it than can be discussed here, but the chief advantage with PCRE is its flexibility and power, which goes well beyond what regular expressions can do. The downside is the great deal of complexity and ambiguity that can be involved.

Introduction to grep-Relevant Environment Variables

In previous examples, we came across the concept of environment variables and their effect on *grep*. Environment variables allow you to customize the default options and behavior of *grep* by defining the environment settings of the shell, thereby making your life easier. Issue an *env* command in a terminal to output all the current parameters. The following is an example of what you might see:

```
$ env
USER=user
LOGNAME=user
HOME=/home/user
PATH=/usr/local/sbin:/usr/local/bin:/usr
/sbin:/usr/bin:/sbin:/bin:/usr/X11R6/bin:.
SHELL=/usr/local/bin/tcsh
OSTYPE=linux
LS_COLORS=no=0:fi=0:di=36:ln=33:ex=32
:bd=0:cd=0:pi=0:so=0:do=0:or=31
VISUAL=vi
EDITOR=vi
MANPATH=/usr/local/man:/usr/man:/usr
/share/man:/usr/X11R6/man
...
```

By manipulating the *.profile* file in your home directory, you can make permanent changes to the variables. For example, using the output just shown, suppose you decide to change your EDITOR from vi to vim. In *.profile*, type:

```
setenv EDITOR vim
```

After writing out the changes, this permanently ensures *vim* will be the default editor for each session that uses this *.profile*. The previous examples use some of the built-in variables, but if you are code-savvy, there is no limit (save for your imagination) on the variables you create and set.

To reiterate, *grep* is a powerful search tool because of the many options available to the user. Variables are no different. There are several specific options, which we describe in detail later. However, it should be noted that *grep* falls back onto C locale when the variables LC_*foo*, LC_ALL, or LANG are not set, when the local catalog is not installed, or when the national language support (NLS) is not complied.

To start off, "locale" is the convention used for communicating in a particular language. For example, when you set the variable LANG or language to English, you are using the conventions tied in with the English language for interacting with the system. When the computer starts up, it defaults to the conventions set up in the kernel, but these settings can be changed.

LC_ALL is not actually a variable, but rather a macro that allows you to "set locale" for all purposes. Although LC_*foo* is a locale-specific setting for a variety of character sets, *foo* can be replaced by ALL, COLLATE, CTYPE, MONETARY, or TIME, to name a few. These are then set to create the overall language conventions for the environment, but it becomes possible to use one language's conventions for money and another for time conventions.

How is this related to *grep*? For instance, many of the POSIX character classes depend on which specific locale is being used. PCRE also borrows heavily from locale settings, especially for the character classes it uses. Because *grep* is designed for searching for text in text files, the way language is processed on a machine matters, and that is determined by the locale.

For most users, leaving the locale settings as the default is fine. Users who wish to search in other languages or want to work in a different language than the system environment might want to change these.

Now that we have familiarized ourselves with the concept of the locale, the environment variables specific to *grep* are:

GREP_OPTIONS

> This variable overrides the "compiled" default options for *grep*. This is as if they were placed in the command line as options themselves. For example, suppose you want to create a variable for the option --binary-files and set it to text. Therefore, --binary-files automatically implies --binary-files=text, without the need to write it out. However, --binary-files can be overridden by specific and different variables (--binary-files=without-match, for example).

> This option is especially useful for scripting, where a set of "default options" can be specified once in the environment variables and it never has to be referenced again. There is one gotcha, though: any options set with GREP_OPTIONS will be interpreted as though they were put on the command line. This means that command-line

options don't override the environment variable, and if they conflict, *grep* will produce an error. For instance:

```
$ export GREP_OPTIONS=-E
$ grep -G '(red)' test
grep: conflicting matchers specified
```

Some care and consideration needs to be taken when putting options into this environment variable, and it is almost always best to set only those options that are of a general nature (for instance, how to handle binary files or devices, whether to use color, etc.).

GREP_COLORS *(or* GREP_COLOR *for older versions)*

This variable specifies the color to be used for highlighting the matching pattern. This is invoked with the --color[=*WHEN*] option, where *WHEN* is never, auto, or always. The setting should be a two-digit number from the list in Table 6 that corresponds to the specific color.

Table 6. List of color options

Color	Color code
Black	0;30
Dark gray	1;30
Blue	0;34
Light blue	1;34
Green	0;32
Light green	1;32
Cyan	0;36
Light cyan	1;36
Red	0;31
Light red	1;31
Purple	0;35
Light purple	1;35
Brown	0;33
Yellow	1;33

Color	Color code
Light gray	0;37
White	1;37

The colors need to be specified in a particular syntax because the highlighting covers additional fields as well, not just matching words. The default setting is as follows:

```
GREP_COLORS='ms=01;31:mc=01;31:sl=:
cx=:fn=35:ln=32:bn=32:se=36'
```

If the desired color starts with 0 (as with 0;30, which is black), the 0 can be discarded to shorten the setting. Where settings are left blank, the default terminal color normal text is used. ms stands for matching string (i.e., the pattern you enter), mc is matching context (i.e., lines shown with the -C option), sl is for the color of selected lines, cx is the color for selected context, fn is the color for the filename (when shown), ln is the color for line numbers (when shown), bn is for byte numbers (when shown), and se is for separator color.

LC_ALL, LC_COLLATE, LANG
These variables have to be specified in that order, but ultimately they determine the collating or an arrangement in the proper sequence of the expressed ranges. For instance, this could be the sequence of letters for alphabetizing.

LC_ALL, LC_CTYPE, LANG
These variables determine LC_CTYPE, or the type of characters to be used by *grep*. For example, which characters are whitespace, which will be a form feed, and so on.

LC_ALL, LC_MESSAGES, LANG
These variables determine the MESSAGES locale and which language *grep* will use for the messages that it outputs. This is a prime example of where *grep* falls back on the C locale's default, which is American English.

POSIXLY_CORRECT

When set, *grep* follows the POSIX.2 requirements that state any options following filenames are treated as filenames themselves. Otherwise, those options are treated as if they are moved before filenames and treated as options. For instance, `grep -E string filename -C 3` would interpret "-C 3" as filenames instead of as an option. Additionally, POSIX.2 states that any unrecognized options be labeled as "illegal"—by default, under GNU *grep*, these are treated as "invalid."

Choosing Between grep Types and Performance Considerations

Now that we have gone over all four *grep* programs, the question is how should you determine which to employ for a given task. For most routine uses, people tend to use the standard *grep* command (*grep -G*) because performance isn't an issue when searching small files and when complex search patterns aren't necessary. Generally, the basic *grep* is the default choice for most people, and so the question becomes when it makes sense to use something else.

When to Use grep -E

Although almost everything can be done in *grep -G* that can be done in *grep -E*, the latter has the advantage of accomplishing the task in fewer characters, without the counterintuitive escaping discussed earlier. All of the extra functionality in extended regular expressions has to do with quantifiers or subpatterns. Additionally, if any significant use of backreferences is needed, extended regular expressions are ideal.

When to Use grep -F

There is one prerequisite to using *grep -F*, and if a user cannot meet that requirement, *grep -F* is simply not an option. Namely, any search pattern for *grep -F* cannot contain any metacharacters, escapes, wildcards, or alternations. Its performance is faster, but at the expense of functionality.

That said, *grep -F* is extremely useful for quickly searching large amounts of data for tightly defined strings, making it the ideal tool to search through immense logfiles quickly. In fact, it is fairly easy to develop a robust "log watching" script with *grep -F* and a good text file listing of important words or phrases that should be pulled out of logfiles for analysis.

Another good use for *grep -F* is searching through mail logs and mail folders to ensure delivery of emails to users, especially on systems with many mail accounts. This is made possible by assigning every email message a unique Message ID. For instance:

```
grep -FHr MESSAGE-ID /var/mail
```

This command will search for the fixed string *MESSAGE-ID* for all files inside */var/mail* (and recurse any subdirectories), and then display the match and also the filename. This is a quick, down-and-dirty way to see which users have a particular message sitting in their mailbox. The real bonus is that this information can be verified without ever having to look inside a user's mailbox and deal with the privacy issues of reading other people's mail. In reality, you may wish to search mailbox directories and spam folders, which typically aren't stored under */var/mail*, but you get the point of how this works.

When to Use grep -P

Perl-style regular expressions are hands-down the most powerful of all the styles presented in this book. They are also the most complicated, prone to user-error, and potentially capable of bogging down a system's performance if not done correctly. However, it is clearly the superior style out of all the regular expression formats used in this book.

For this reason, many applications prefer to use PCRE instead of GNU regular expressions. For instance, the popular intrusion detection system snort uses PCRE to match bad packets on the wire. The patterns are written intelligently so that there can be very little packet loss, even though a single machine can search all the packets going through a fully loaded 100 MB or GB interface. As has been said before, writing a regular expression well tends to be more important than the particular regular expression format you use.

Some people simply prefer to use *grep -P* as their default (for instance, by specifying -P inside their `GREP_OPTIONS` environment variable). If searching is going to be done in an "international" way, the PCRE language character classes make this far easier. PCRE comes with a many more character classes for finely tuning a regular expression, beyond what is possible with the POSIX definitions, for instance. Most importantly, the ability to use the various PCRE options (e.g., `PCRE_MULTILINE`) allows searching in more powerful ways than GNU regular expressions.

For simple to moderately complex regular expressions, *grep -E* suffices. However, there are limitations, and those may push a user toward PCRE. It is a trade-off between complexity and functionality. PCRE also helps users craft regular expressions that can be almost immediately transferred directly into Perl scripts (or transferred from Perl scripts) without having to go through a great deal of translation.

Performance Implications

For most routine uses, *grep* performance is not an issue. Even megabyte-long files can be searched quickly using any of the specific *grep* programs without any noticeable performance difference. Obviously, the larger the file, the longer the search takes. For searching through gigabytes or terabytes of data when performance is a consideration, *grep -F* is likely the desired solution, but only if it is possible to craft the search pattern without using any metacharacters, alternations, or backreferences. This is not always the case.

The more "choices" given to *grep*, the longer a particular search takes. For instance, using many alternations causes *grep* to search lines multiple times instead of just once. This may be necessary for a given search pattern, but occasionally alternation can be rewritten as a character class. For instance:

```
grep -E '(0|2|4|6|8)' filename
grep -E '[02468]' filename
```

Comparing the two examples, the second one performs better because no alternation is used and so lines do not have to be searched multiple times. Avoid alternation when other alternatives exist that accomplish the same thing.

By far, the biggest cause of performance slowdowns when using *grep* is the use of backreferences. The time it takes *grep* to run a command increases almost exponentially with the use of additional backreferences. Backreferences can, in effect, become handy aliases to previous subpatterns; however, performance will suffer. Backreferences should not be used if performance is a concern and when subpatterns are not using alternation for this reason. See the next section for a more detailed discussion of backreferences.

In closing, among *grep -G*, *grep -E*, and *grep -P*, there is not much of a performance impact; it depends mostly on how the regular expression itself is constructed. That said, *grep -P* provides the most opportunities for slower performance but also the most flexibility to match a wide variety of content.

Advanced Tips and Tricks with grep

As mentioned earlier, *grep* can be used in very powerful ways to search for content in files or across a filesystem. It is possible to use previous matches to search later strings (called backreferences). There are also a variety of tricks to search nonpublic personal information and even find binary strings in binary files. The following sections discuss some advanced tips and tricks.

Backreferences

The *grep* program has the ability to match based on multiple previous conditions. For instance, if you want to find all lines that repeatedly use a particular set of words, a single *grep* pattern will not work; however, it is possible to do this with the use of backreferences.

Suppose you wish to find any line that has multiple instances of the words "red", "blue", or "green". Imagine the following text file:

```
The red dog fetches the green ball.
The green dog fetches the blue ball.
The blue dog fetches the blue ball.
```

Only the third line repeats the use of the same color. A regular expression pattern of ''(red|green|blue)*(red|green|blue)'' would return all three lines. To overcome this problem, you could use backreferences:

```
grep -E '(red|green|blue).*\1' filename
```

This command matches only the third line, as intended. For extended regular expressions, only a single digit can be used to specify a backreference (i.e., you can only refer back to the ninth backreference). Using Perl-style regular expressions, theoretically you can have many more (at least two digits).

This could be used to validate XML syntax (i.e., the "opening" and "closing" tags are the same), HTML syntax (match all lines with the various opening and closing "heading" tags, such as <h1>, <h2>, etc.), or even to analyze writing for pointless repetition of buzzwords.

It is important to note that backreferences require the use of parentheses to determine reference numbers. *grep* will read the search pattern from left to right, and starting with the first parenthetical subpattern it finds, it will start numbering from 1.

Typically, backreferences are used when a subpattern contains alternation, as in the previous example. It is not required, however, for a subpattern to actually contain alternation. For instance, assuming there is a large subpattern that you wish to refer back to later in the regular expression, you could use a backreference as an artificial "alias" for that subpattern without having to type out the entire pattern multiple times. For instance:

```
grep -E '(I am the very model of a
modern major general.).*\1' filename
```

would search for repetitions of the sentence "I am the very model of a modern major general." separated by any amount of optional content. This certainly reduces the number of keystrokes and makes the regular expression more manageable, but it also causes some performance considerations as discussed previously. The user needs to weigh the benefits of convenience with performance, depending on what she is trying to accomplish.

Binary File Searching

Up to this point, it seems that *grep* could only be used to search for text strings in text files. This is what it is most used for, but *grep* can also search for strings in binary files.

It is important to note that "text" files exist on computers mostly for human readability. Computers talk purely in binary and machine code. The entire ASCII character set consists of 255 characters, of which only about 60 are "human-readable." However, many computer programs contain text strings as well. For instance, "help" screens, filenames, error messages, and expected user input may appear as text inside binary files.

The *grep* command does not distinguish to any great extent between searching text or binary files. As long as you feed it patterns (even binary patterns), it will happily search any file for the patterns you tell it to search. It does do an initial check to see if a file is binary and alters the way it displays results accordingly (unless you manually specify other behavior):

```
bash$ grep help /bin/ls
Binary file /bin/ls matches
```

This command searches for the string "help" in the binary file
ls. Instead of showing the line where the text appears, it simply
indicates that a match was found. The reason again relates to
the fact that computer programs are in binary and therefore
not human-readable. There are no "lines" in programs, for instance. Binary files don't add line breaks because they would
alter the code—they are simply a feature to make text files more
readable, which is why *grep* tells you only whether there is a
match. To get an idea of the kind of text that is in a binary file,
you can use the *strings* command. For instance, `strings /bin/`
`ls` would list all the text strings in the *ls* command.

There is another way to search binary files that is specific for
binary data as well. In this case, you need to rely on some tricks,
because you cannot type in binary data directly with a normal
keyboard. Instead, you need to use a special form of a regular
expression to type in the hexadecimal equivalent of the data
you want to search. For instance, if you wanted to search a
binary file that had a hexadecimal string of ABAA, you would
type the following command:

```
bash$ grep '[\xabaa]' test.hex
Binary file test.hex matches
```

The general format is to type /x and then the hexadecimal
string you wish to match. There is no real limit to the size of
the string you can enter. This type of searching could be useful
in malware analysis. For instance, the metasploit framework
(*http://www.metasploit.org*) can generate binary payloads to
exploit remote machines. This payload could be used to
establish a remote shell, add accounts, or accomplish other
malicious activity.

Using hexadecimal searching, it would be possible to determine from binary strings which of the metasploit payloads
were being used in an actual attack. Additionally, if you could
determine a unique hexadecimal string that was used in a virus,
you could create a basic virus scanner using *grep*. In fact, many

older virus scanners did more or less this very thing by searching for unique binary strings in files against a list of known bad hexadecimal signatures.

Many buffer overflows or exploit payloads are written in C, and it is typical to write out each hexadecimal digit in C with the \x escape. For instance, take the following buffer overflow exploit payload:

```
"\xeb\x17\x5e\x89\x76\x08\x31\xc0\x88\x46
\x07\x89\x46\x0c\xb0\x0b\x89\xf3\x8d\x4e
\x08\x31\xd2\xcd\x80\xe8\xe4\xff\xff\xff
\x2f\x62\x69\x6e\x2f\x73\x68\x58";
```

It may be more advantageous to write the regular expression in the same way instead of typing out the entire hexadecimal string, if for no other reason than to allow for copying and pasting from exploit code. Either way could work—it is your preference. The exploit just shown works against Red Hat 5 and 6 machines (not Enterprise Red Hat), so this particular code is useless, but it is not hard to find exploit code in the wild.

As an interesting aside, this method does not seem to work for searching files that are recognized as text files. For instance, if you tried to search for text in a text file using the hexadecimal equivalent of the ASCII codes, *grep* would not find the content. Searching for hexadecimal strings works only for files that *grep* recognizes as "binary."

Useful Recipes

The following is a quick list of useful *grep* recipes to find certain classes of content. Because the availability of Perl-based regular expressions varies, the list will use extended *grep*-style recipes, even though Perl would be quicker in many cases.

Typing these commands in on the command line and returning the default output to the screen may not make much sense if the desire is to search for sensitive information on a partition. It would make more sense to use the -l and -r options to recurse through an entire filesystem and display matching filenames instead of entire lines.

For many recipes, it makes sense to place \b before and after the string. This ensures that the content has some sort of whitespace before and after it, preventing the case in which you are looking for a 9-digit number that appears to be a Social Security number but get false-positive matches on 29-digit numbers.

Finally, these patterns (and potentially others that may make sense) can be put into a file and used as a list of input patterns given to *grep*, so all of them are searched for at the same time.

IP addresses

```
$ grep -E '\b[0-9]{1,3}(\.[0-9]{1,3}){3}
\b' patterns

123.24.45.67
312.543.121.1
```

This pattern will help point out IP addresses in a file. It is important to note that [0-9] could have just as easily been replaced with [:digit:] for better readability. However, most users tend to prefer less keystrokes compared to readability when given the choice. A second note is that this will also find strings that aren't valid IP addresses, such as the second one listed in the example. Regular expressions work on individual characters, and there is not a good way to tell *grep* to search for a range of values from 1–255. In this case, there may be false positives. A more complicated formula to ensure that false positives are not registered looks like:

```
$ grep -E '\b((25[0-5]|2[0-4][0-9]|[01]?
[0-9][0-9]?)\.){3}(25[0-5]|2[0-4][0-9]|
[01]?[0-9][0-9]?)\b' patterns
```

In this case, it makes sure to find IP addresses with an octet between 0–255 by establishing a combination of patterns that would work. This does guarantee only matching IP addresses, but it is more complicated and has lower performance.

MAC addresses

```
$ grep -Ei '\b[0-9a-f]{2}
(:[0-9a-f]{2}){5}\b' patterns

ab:14:ed:41:aa:00
```

In this case, the additional -i option is added so no regard is given to capitalization. As with the IP recipe, [:xdigit:] could be used in place of [0-9a-f] if better readability is desired.

Email addresses

```
$ grep -Ei '\b[a-z0-9]{1,}@*\.
(com|net|org|uk|mil|gov|edu)\b' patterns

test@some.com
test@some.edu
test@some.co.uk
```

The list shown here is only a partial subset of top-level domains that are currently approved for use. For instance, one may wish to search for only U.S.-based addresses, so the *.uk* result may not make much sense. Perhaps identifying obvious spammers in the mail logs is the goal, in which case searching for the *.info* top-level domain may be advised (we have never met anyone who has gotten legitimate email from that top-level domain). The pattern shown is basically a starting point for customization.

U.S.-based phone numbers

```
$ grep -E '\b(\(|\|)[0-9]{3}
(\)|-|\)-|)[0-9]{3}(-|)[0-9]{4}\b'
 patterns

(312)-555-1212
(312) 555-1212
312-555-1212
3125551212
```

In this case, the pattern is a little more complex because of the wide variety of U.S.-based phone numbers. There may be spaces, dashes, parentheses, or nothing at all. Note the way the parentheses indicate the presence of varying characters, including no character at all.

Social Security numbers

```
$ grep -E '\b[0-9]{3}( |-|)
[0-9]{2}( |-|)[0-9]{4}\b' patterns

333333333
333 33 3333
333-33-3333
```

Social Security numbers are the key to an individual's identity in the United States, so the use of this identifier is becoming increasingly restricted. Many organizations now actively search all files on a system for Social Security numbers using tools such as Spider. This tool is not much more sophisticated than a list of these *grep* recipes. In this case, however, the pattern is far simpler than the one for phone numbers.

Credit card numbers

For most credit card numbers, this expression works:

```
$ grep -E '\b[0-9]{4}(( |-|)
[0-9]{4}){3}\b' patterns

1234 5678 9012 3456
1234567890123456
1234-5678-9012-3456
```

American Express card numbers would be caught by this expression:

```
$ grep -E '\b[0-9]{4}( |-|)
[0-9]{6}( |-|)[0-9]{5}\b' patterns

1234-567890-12345
123456789012345
1234 567890 12345
```

There are two versions because American Express uses a different pattern than other credit cards. However, the basic idea remains the same: looking for groupings of numbers that fit the general pattern of a credit card number.

Copyright-protected or confidential material

Finally, many organizations have internal data classifications that make it easy to identify privileged information within an organization. Hopefully, these data classifications come with required text that must be displayed in the document. Those strings can simply be put in as search patterns in *grep* (or *fgrep*) to quickly identify where protected information may reside on a disk, especially on those machines where that information does not belong.

Most file formats with text are not true ASCII files, but usually the text content can be located and identified within the file. For instance, you can use *grep* to search for the presence of certain strings in Word files, even though these files aren't viewable in a terminal.

For instance, if your corporation uses the tag "ACME Corp.—Proprietary and Confidential," you could use the following command to locate files that have this content:

```
fgrep -l 'ACME Corp. -
Proprietary and Confidential' patterns
```

Searching through large numbers of files

Like many shell commands, the *grep* command will process a large number of files in a given command. For instance, *grep sometext* * will examine every filename in the current directory for "sometext". However, there is a limit to the number of files that can be handled in a single command. If you ask *grep* to process too many files, it will produce an error saying "Too Many Files" or the equivalent (depending on your shell).

A tool called *xargs* can get around this limitation. To invoke it, however, requires some circumspection. For instance, to search every file on a system for "ABCDEFGH", you would use the following command:

```
find / -print | xargs grep 'ABCDEFGH'
```

This will search every file on a machine for the string "ABCDEFGH", but will not run into the typical errors that result when too many files are open. Usually this limit is a function of the kernel that allows only so many pages of memory to be devoted to command-line arguments. Short of recompiling the kernel for a larger value, using *xargs* is your best bet.

Matching strings across multiple lines

At the start of this book, we said that *grep* cannot match strings if they span multiple lines, but that isn't precisely true. Although most versions of *grep* cannot handle multiple lines easily, *grep -P* can overcome this in multiline mode. For instance, take the following file:

```
red
dog
```

Normal *grep* tricks, even specifying the newline character, will not match if you want to search for a line with "red" and the following line "dog".

```
$ grep -E 'red\ndog' test
$ grep -G 'red\ndog' test
$ grep -F 'red\ndog' test
```

However, this is possible if you use `PCRE_MULTILINE` with *grep -P*:

```
$ grep -P '(?m)red\ndog' test
red
dog
```

This allows a user to overcome the limitation in *grep* where it will examine only individual lines. This is also one of the many reasons why *grep -P* tends to be used for more powerful searching applications.

Finally, there are many websites and forums out there where you can find useful regular expression patterns for particular applications. Odds are that others have used regular expressions and *grep* to pull content out of that same application. The possibilities are endless.

References

- re_format(7) manpage
- regex(3) manpage
- grep(1) manpage
- pcre(3) manpage
- pcrepattern(3) manpage
- Friedl, Jeffery E.F. (2006). *Mastering Regular Expressions*. O'Reilly Media, Inc.

Index

Symbols

" (double quotes), using
   regular expressions
   and, 9
$ (dollar sign), end of line
   character, 10, 14
' (single quotes), using regular
   expressions, 8
( ) (parentheses)
   extended regular
      expressions, 40
   precedence in regular
      expressions, 22
   subpatterns, 19
( ) parentheses, 10
* (asterisk) quantifier, 8, 10,
   15
+ (plus) quantifier, 10, 18
   extended regular
      expressions and, 39
- (dashes), indicating ranges,
   10, 15

. (dot), 10, 12
> (redirects), 24
? (question mark) quantifier,
   10, 17
   optional expressions, 38
[...] (character classes), 10,
   12
[^...] (negated character
   class), 10, 13
\ (backslashes), 11, 16, 40
\ escape characters, 10, 11,
   13
\' (end of buffer), 11, 17
\< (backslash less-than), 10
\< (start of word), 14
\> (backslash greater-than),
   10
\> (end of word), 15
\` (start of buffer), 11, 17
^ (caret), as a start of line, 9,
   10, 14
` (backticks), 8
{min,max} quantifier, 10

We'd like to hear your suggestions for improving our indexes. Send email to
index@oreilly.com.

D

\d (decimal digit) character, 45

\D (non-decimal) character, 45

\d escape sequence, 27

-D flag, 35

-d flag, 35

dashes (-), indicating ranges, 10, 15

decimal digit (\d) character, 45

--devices option, 35

[:digit:] POSIX definition, 20

--directories option, 35

--disable-perl-regexp configuration, 44

dollar sign ($), end of line character, 10, 14

dot (.), 10, 12

double quotes ("), using regular expressions and, 9

E

-e flag, 28
  fgrep, 42

-E option, 38–41, 54

\e PCRE escape, 45

egrep, 38–41, 40

email addresses, 63

--enable-unicode-properties configuration option, 48

end of buffer (\'), 11, 17

end of line ($) character, 10, 14

end of word (\>), 15

env command, 49

environment variables, 49–54

escape characters, 10, 11, 13

escape sequences (regular expressions), 8

--exclude option, 36

--exclude-dir option, 36

--exclude-from option, 36

extended regular expressions, 38–41

F

\f (form feed) PCRE escape, 45

-f flag, 28
  fgrep, 42

-F option, 41–43, 55
  performance implications and, 56

Fedora operating system, 44

--file option, 28

files, searching, 6

--files-with-matches option, 30

--files-without-match option, 30

flags, 27–38
  general output control, 29–32

form feed (\f) PCRE escape, 45

Free Software Foundation, 1

G

\G character, 46

-G option, 27–38, 54

mmap( ) function, 37
more command, 24

N

\n (newline) PCRE escape, 45
-n flag, 33
    fgrep, 43
{N,} quantifier, 10, 18
national language support
    (NLS), 50
negated character class
    ([^...]), 10, 13
newline (\n) PCRE escape, 45
NLS (national language
    support), 50
--no-filename option, 32
--no-messages option, 31
non-decimal (\D) character,
    45
non-whitespace (\S)
    character, 45
non-word character (\W), 11,
    17, 45
--null option, 33
--null-data option, 38
{N} quantifier, 10, 18

O

-o flag, 31
octal searching, 46
--only-matching option, 31
optional expression (?), 38
"optional" pattern matching,
    17
Oracle, 7
output control, 29–32

P

-P option, 43–49, 55
parentheses (( )), 10
    extended regular
        expressions, 40
    precedence in regular
        expressions, 22
    subpatterns, 19
PCRE (Perl-Compatible
    Regular Expressions),
    43, 46
    character properties, 46
    octal searching, 46
    options, 48
    when to use, 56
pcre manpage, 44
pcrepattern, 47
pcrepattern manpage, 44
PCRE_CASELESS (i), 48
PCRE_DOTALL (s), 48
PCRE_EXTENDED (x), 48
PCRE_MULTILINE (m), 48
Perl-Compatible Regular
    Expressions (PCRE),
    43, 46
    character properties, 46
    options, 48
    when to use, 56
Perl-style regular expressions,
    7, 43–49
    backreferences and, 58
    octal searching, 46
    when to use, 55
phone numbers, 63
pipe (|), 10, 19
    chaining commands and,
        25

T

\t (tab) character, 45
-T flag, 33
tab (\t) character, 45
target strings, 8
text files, searching, 6
--text option, 34
tput init command, 35
tput reset command, 35

U

-u flag, 33
-U option, 37
U.S.-based phone numbers, 63
--unix-byte-offsets option, 33
[:upper:] POSIX definition, 20

V

-v flag, 28
   fgrep, 43
-V flag, 38
--version option, 38

W

\W (non-word character), 11, 17, 45
\w (word character), 11, 17, 45
-w flag, 29
whitespace (\s) character, 45
whoami command, 8, 23
wildcards, 8, 10, 15
   --exclude option, 36
Windows, 1

wingrep, 1
--with-filename option, 32
word boundary (\b), 11, 16, 46
word character (\w), 11, 17, 45
--word-regexp option, 29

X

x (PCRE_EXTENDED), 48
\x excape, 61
-x flag, 29
   fgrep, 43
[:xdigit:] POSIX definition, 20

Z

\Z character, 46
\z character, 46
-Z flag, 33
-z flag, 38
zipgrep, 2

Get even more for your money.

Join the O'Reilly Community, and register the O'Reilly books you own. It's free, and you'll get:

- $4.99 ebook upgrade offer
- 40% upgrade offer on O'Reilly print books
- Membership discounts on books and events
- Free lifetime updates to ebooks and videos
- Multiple ebook formats, DRM FREE
- Participation in the O'Reilly community
- Newsletters
- Account management
- 100% Satisfaction Guarantee

Registering your books is easy:
1. **Go to: oreilly.com/go/register**
2. **Create an O'Reilly login.**
3. **Provide your address.**
4. **Register your books.**

Note: English-language books only

To order books online:
oreilly.com/store

For questions about products or an order:
orders@oreilly.com

To sign up to get topic-specific email announcements and/or news about upcoming books, conferences, special offers, and new technologies:
elists@oreilly.com

For technical questions about book content:
booktech@oreilly.com

To submit new book proposals to our editors:
proposals@oreilly.com

O'Reilly books are available in multiple DRM-free ebook formats. For more information:
oreilly.com/ebooks

O'REILLY®

Spreading the knowledge of innovators   oreilly.com

The information you need, when and where you need it.

With Safari Books Online, you can:

Access the contents of thousands of technology and business books

- Quickly search over 7000 books and certification guides
- Download whole books or chapters in PDF format, at no extra cost, to print or read on the go
- Copy and paste code
- Save up to 35% on O'Reilly print books
- **New!** Access mobile-friendly books directly from cell phones and mobile devices

Stay up-to-date on emerging topics before the books are published

- Get on-demand access to evolving manuscripts.
- Interact directly with authors of upcoming books

Explore thousands of hours of video on technology and design topics

- Learn from expert video tutorials
- Watch and replay recorded conference sessions

O'REILLY®

Spreading the knowledge of innovators | oreilly.com

CPSIA information can be obtained
at www.ICGtesting.com
Printed in the USA
BVOW10s0601060917
494013BV00009B/17/P